Adva
Thanks for Letting

"A kaleidoscopic book that performs grief's tireless and ambitious work, Jennifer Tseng's poems, aptly narrowed and scalpel-shaped, concussive with enjambment and hard stops, commit to the work of excavation and salvage—but do so via the heartbreaking and heart filled collaboration with the dead and the ghosts that go on living in our words. A clear-eyed and courageous feat."

—Ocean Vuong, author of *Time Is a Mother* and
On Earth We're Briefly Gorgeous

"Jennifer Tseng's *Thanks for Letting Us Know You Are Alive* asks: what do we remember if we go further, and further still? Pulling from the exoskeleton of the speaker's father's letters, these poems worm their way through memory, language, childhood, and diaspora, creating new epistolary creatures: "Love rid itself / Then led me here." Deeply intimate, these poems pulsate with grief and terror, as well as tenderness toward the healing self. Each fragment, each line break is gorgeously considered, as each ghost unfurls with complicated longing: 'My ghost, my guessed. / Where are you, farther?'"

—Jane Wong, author of *Meet Me Tonight in Atlantic City* and
How to Not Be Afraid of Everything

"Distinguished by italics, the language lifted from these letters takes on an eerie physicality; I feel I can touch English as it swells, ripples, shines, and breathes. *Thanks for Letting Us Know You Are Alive* is a radiant reminder that we are all children of someone or something gone, sifting through and integrating the language the human dead leave in their wake: 'Like you, I died & became / English words . . . Your words are my sisters.' Its commanding speaker faces with grace and verve the infinite mysteries and pressures of blood relation. This book is at once an intoxicating page-turner and an intricate lyric investigation of correspondence under global capitalism. I will cherish it."

—Emily R. Hunt, author of *Company* and *Dark Green*

"Crackling with the charge of the unsayable, *Thanks for Letting Us Know You Are Alive* is a richly moving collection that unseams entanglements and griefs from a father's pained correspondence. Tseng bends, warps, and undercuts the language of these letters to build a blooming and intimate work that evokes the distances and hauntings between us and our closest relations. Through Tseng's arresting play of language, these poems enact a stunning dance of loss and retrieval, and of the many ways in which 'a father never ends.'"

—Jenny Xie, author of *Eye Level* and *The Rupture Tense*

"Jennifer Tseng's *Thanks for Letting Us Know You Are Alive* braids silence and grief, intergenerational trauma and personal memory. These poems and hymns show the many faces of language, from what could have been to what is now possible. Tseng spares no words for the neglected plant which flowers anyway. The intimate letters from a father press firmly into the page, holding worlds of duty, alarm, failure, and unbearable love."

—E. J. Koh, author of *The Magical Language of Others* and
A Lesser Love

"The speaker of Jennifer Tseng's *Thanks for Letting Us Know You Are Alive* is a speaker deeply attuned to both the harm and the healing that language can do. Drawing on language from a father/phantom's letters, the daughter/darer of these poems reconstructs adolescence, deconstructs diaspora, and gorgeously makes song out of sorrow. These poems sing and sting. A father's appeal becomes a daughter's appall; university morphs into universal; Diane turns out to be Diana; to remember is to 'member it again / & again,' to 'dream the embers of a hooded / nation into place'; and two people can and do share a face—'Every morning I see / You mourning in the mirror.' Jennifer Tseng reminds us of the power of address, the dangers and the liberations of the epistolary. These poems made me weep and ravenously wonder."

—Chen Chen, author of *Your Emergency Contact Has
Experienced an Emergency*

Thanks for Letting Us Know You Are Alive

Thanks for Letting Us Know You Are Alive

POEMS

JENNIFER TSENG

UNIVERSITY OF MASSACHUSETTS PRESS
Amherst and Boston

Copyright © 2024 by University of Massachusetts Press
All rights reserved
Printed in the United States of America

ISBN 978-1-62534-808-1 (paper)

Designed by Sally Nichols
Set in Adobe Jenson Pro
Printed and bound by Books International, Inc.

Cover design and art by Sally Nichols
Cover art by Sydney Acosta, *Strawberries,* detail, oil & spray paint on canvas,
78 x 96, 2021. From the collection of Nithya Raman. Courtesy of the artist.
Instagram: @theofficialsydneyacosta

Library of Congress Cataloging-in-Publication Data

Names: Tseng, Jennifer, author.
Title: Thanks for letting us know you are alive / Jennifer Tseng.
Description: Amherst : University of Massachusetts Press, 2024. | Series:
    Juniper prize for poetry | Identifiers: LCCN 2023046514 (print) | LCCN 2023046515
(ebook) | ISBN
    9781625348081 (paperback) | ISBN 9781685750794 (ebook)
Subjects: LCGFT: Poetry.
Classification: LCC PS3620.S46 T47 2024 (print) | LCC PS3620.S46 (ebook)
    | DDC 811/.6—dc23/eng/20231013
LC record available at https://lccn.loc.gov/2023046514
LC ebook record available at https://lccn.loc.gov/2023046515

British Library Cataloguing-in-Publication Data
A catalog record for this book is available from the British Library.

曾献文

1925-2007

My father is better than your father.
My father is the best father.

CONTENTS

I. Not

II. So

III. Dear

He who does the work gives birth to his own father.

—from Søren Kierkegaard, *Fear and Trembling*,
translator unknown

Italicized phrases & sentences come from my father's letters, written to me between 1984 & 2007.

Thanks for Letting Us Know You Are Alive

I. Not

Not so dear Jenny:

We sew a knot
To hold the thing
That's *dear* to us.
Ropes that lashed
Your trunk to the mast,
Cord that fastened
Your briefcase to the bicycle,
Thread at the end of the seam
Down the back of my dress.
Eleven letters to confess
Your love. Three more
To negate it.
Not so, dear Jenny,
Not so.
That knot.
Our fear,
So dear
Is its undoing.

But we two can never divorce each other.

The longing to marry your father,
Expressed in two languages,
Doubles the feeling.
The ocean between you
Elongates the longing.
As a child I wanted to go
To the pyramids, to Egypt, to outer space.
Without knowing I was waiting,
I waited & waited.
There was no proposal.
He married someone else.
Someone who smiled a lot
Whose scorn was palpable.
When he died, she vanished.
Every time he said, *We two*
Can never divorce each other,
I wanted to leave him.
Every time he said, *We two*
Can never divorce each other,
I wanted to stay with him forever.
I looked for someone else to marry.
I developed a fondness for people
Who pretended to be my father.
It was a very exciting time.
Some of my best fathers were women.
In the end I married a replica of my sister.
If he wasn't going to marry me,
I wasn't going to marry him either.
Every night, I sleep
In the arms of my child
While he sleeps in his grave.
But we two can never divorce each other.

Dear Jenny:

The intimate

Feeling is difficult

To cultivate without

Living closely together.

I am your daddy.

The reality is cruel.

Parents do not understand us.

Nights and days we work for them.

Then everything starts over again.

"Please say hi to your family for me."

Not words
A Chinese girl
Writes *to* her father.
You put my nots in nooses,
You buttoned *your* ancient coat.
Your letter lynched my letters,
The sentence cinched & hung
By the mast that made *me*.
A master nod *to* days of yore
When *yours* & mine were one &
Lost at sea. I would write
All my problems down
& come *to your* study.
You'd withhold the answers.
You were alone with knowledge.
It lived in the hold of you.
You held it.
Answer it yourself, you'd *say*.
Answer it yourself!
When I found the *answer*,
I tried not *to* laugh,
Not *to* undo myself
In front of you. I tried
To be knowledge
Or sailor
But I was sea.
Tide & untied.

Oh, that was quite a letter.

My alphabet
Kite trailed you
Along the shore.
She knew
Failure to soar.
She knew
Fight & flight,
She knew
Being watched
From afar,
At *a* great height.
A blue sky
A gray sky
A black one.
She knew
Being held
By so slender
A string, *a* strand
In your hand,
So long
Out of sight.
She didn't know
Her own weight
Because you never
Let go.
You thought
A daughter
Was *a* kite
You had
To hold.

Please let me know how you feel about this
understanding. Can you take it or you can
care less.

I can take it.
Like criticism.
Like a beating.
A free pamphlet
Or someone's place.
A stale pastry I stuff
Down my coat.
I'm hungry
& I *can care less.*
I *can care* more.
What meter measures
The things we *care* for?
Not what but *how* much?
Not touch but feeling.
Can you care less
Where *you* are
Can you care more?
Is there more in store of your
Hair & fingernail feelings?
I appreciate your *please.*
It makes *you* seem
Willing to listen.
Such silence *you* have
Granted us. Your
Silence is not taken for
Granted. *How I feel about this*
Understanding is a question.
How can I let you know?

*All of a sudden it dooms on me . . . maybe you
already knew.*

The past can be *sudden.*
What's *already* happened,
What you *already knew,*
Someone who's *already* dead—
Dooms so large they still
Feel forthcoming.
Crimes *on* the horizon,
A rime of frost *on* the rind
Of the melon of your summer.
Zoom lens *on* the magnificent.
Your horror of Zen magnified.
They tell *you* to shut your senses
But *you* won't. *You're not done.*

Parents love for their children has no condition.

Every letter riddled
With *conditions.*
Love rid itself
Then led me here.
It let me.
Every line a riddle.
A very linear id; a baby.
A contradiction
Against speech,
Against tradition.
Impeached again.
Nothing to gain
But the fruit of him.
The stone within.

Do NOT try any sleeping pills under any circumstances.

Strategic use of capital letters.
Tendency to command.
Fondness for warning.
Aversion to affirmation.
Preoccupation with health.
Desire to preserve consciousness.
Fear of a loss of control.
Fear of addiction.
Fear of overdose.
Fear of medicine.
Fear of death.
To inherit
Line after line
Continuously
Is the inherent dilemma.
My inheritance in
A line.
A skirt that flatters
My feelings. Closet
Of skirted meanings,
Of sheep's clothing,
Hoops to jump through
For the night. Sleepless
In the den & counting.

Dear Stranger,

These were worse
Than the labels
Pressed to his letters
By *strangers*,
By machines.
He was in a rage
When he wrote them.
Each word a smudge of
Poison at the top of the page,
Written by a hand that had been
Contaminated, in a hand
I could die from touching.

Love, Your poor and ignored daddy.

A fragment of a list
Of overrated phenomena,
World's greatest mysteries,
Perpetual sources of guilt,
Things a child dreams of having,
Reasons to avoid reading a letter,
Reasons to read a letter,
Explanations for suicide,
Reasons to live.

Why should we blame others for forgetting me?

We is you & *me*
Against the *others*
Who are all of us.
Me is separate.
Me is *blame*less.
Me is forgotten.
I, too, am nowhere to be found.
Like you, I died & became
English words. *We* were
Ruled, punished,
Beaten. You mastered
The language, Father.
You did to them
What you did to *me*.
Your words are my sisters.

Do not second guess my true feeling.

For a firstborn
To *second guess*
Is forbidden.
I am bidden
To avoid being next
After the first.
To avoid meaning
Two in a sequence.
Two is less than one.
Try to be perfect.
Try to be first.
Be *my* guest.
Your *feeling* is *true*.
Our past is a church,
Your letters, the last
Surviving ordinal.
I confess *my* errors,
My ghost, *my guess*ed.
Where are you, farther?
Give me one *guess*.
No, give me two.
Give me more than one
Second with you.

I sincerely hope it was not a decision derived from
the physiological desire of your body.

Why fly anywhere
If *not* to lift *the body*
Into air?
I sincerely hope
To meet you there.
It was not a decision.
It was not derived.
It was not riven
From desire. Tireless,
Your letters arrived
With their *body of* logic.
You de-siring *yourself*
A little more each time.

*Diane is here and we are happy to have her
with us.*

I had forgotten she lived
In our childhood home.
Lay in the same bed
Where I lay
Waiting for a knock
On my window,
For someone *to* climb in.
Maybe she touched *her*self
There, in the same place
Where someone touched me
Then rose *&* crossed the hall
To wash *her* hands.
Back in bed, through the wall
She could hear
My father *& her* mother
Turning over *&* over
In my parents' old bed,
Then silence.
I didn't envy *her.*
I didn't want *her*
There either. My
Petty consolation
Came years later,
Reading his letters.
Her name was Diana,
Not *Diane.*

Dear Jenny & Mandy,

Like the flowers or trees

I grow a plant.

I've neglected to water

Or take care of them

And have no right to complain.

Why are there so many weeds,

Why are they so withered?

As a matter of fact, your daddy is the biggest failure
of you all—I could not even hold a family of four
together!

Facts *mattered* to him.
We were *all big failures.*
He was *the biggest.*
He *couldn't hold* us *together*
Because he couldn't let go
His jaunty rhetoric.
Cunning like silver
*Hold*ing the pearl
In the handle *of a* knife.
They said *I* was just like him.
He called me First Son.
He called me Number One.
They called me *Daddy's* Girl.
He was *the* silver &
I was the pearl &
The blade was life.
We were all one weapon.

To my beloved girl in paradise:

I thought she is just like you

All by herself on an island.

You are almost living

Like a hermit.

I sometimes wonder

What is your ultimate goal—

Fame, money or what.

I couldn't help pondering this

All day on my bed at night.

None of the literature Nobel Prize winners
I know of were graduated from the most
prestigious universities.

None. Comfort or
Come to *the* fort for
Your punishment. Bend
Down on *the* common
Ground *of* our lousy
Origins to be whipped.
Your Honor, no bell will
Ring when *I* prise you
Out *of the* frozen ground.
It's not hot as hell in California,
But you're there, putting down
Roots. You winners are underfoot,
Graduated from the most prestigious
Universal. Me, *I'm* walking,
Crushing leaves with my boots—
Just another loser breathing air.

(*Please note the jade is a genuine jade, not a plastic fake.*)

Inside *the* first word
There's *a* lease
I have yet to sign.
If you genuflect
I may make *note* of it.
Elastic enough to fit *the* ache,
The blade *is a genuine* blade,
Not a plastic fake.
You can use it to cut steak
& pound cake & human hearts.
Your parenthetical has been *noted*, as has
The authenticity of your gift.
Its dog shape, its red string.
Please note the everything
Is a genuine everything
Not a plastic fake.
Like the *jade*, it
Has been *noted*
& came at *a* cost.
Like *the jade,*
It was *not* taken,
But has been lost.

Dear Monkey #1:

I am your father and you are my daughter.

Please keep this in mind as you read.

Please be patient.

This is not a logically developed letter.

I never had a feeling of completion.

I thought I would rearrange

What I wrote at the end.

But time is running out.

I am terribly sorry

For failing to be

Your role model.

I believe

You two deserve

Someone better . . .

I have been

A total failure

As a father . . .

I begged her not to do it.

Such tear-stained letters.
At every party, from any room,
We could hear his laughter
Booming above the others'.
Our mother's silence
Was equal *to* his laughter,
To the letters she never wrote.
Their twin disguise,
Discrepancy, is a dress
That surprises me with
Its functionality. *I* wear *it*
Discreetly, when we meet.

*I would have hated myself for not calling or writing
you more often when I see the Saint at the Gate.*

But *I* didn't die that time.
I promised to *call* & *write*
You more often & I did.
In *the* end, when *I* saw
The Saint at the Gate,
I didn't *hate myself.*
I'd kept my promise.
The Gate was small &
Wooden, faintly familiar.
You remember. It was
A duplicate, *I* believe.
There was no one else
Under *the* archway
Of leaves. *I* cried
When *I* saw her. Stranger
With a plaintiff's face
Who couldn't erase
The letters *I* wrote,
The phones that rang,
The years *I* spent waiting
For you to answer.
It began with *the Saint*
Seeing me *see* this.

II. So

Now you have completely disappeared.

He kept writing me letters.
I moved to the mountains.
I moved to the woods.
I moved to a small town.   .
I moved to another country.
I moved to a foreign city.
I moved to a series of islands.

With each letter
I *disappeared*
A little further
From my father
Into the world.

When he died I began
The return journey.   .
I kept reading his letters.
I remembered the mountains.
I remembered the woods.
I remembered the small town.
I remembered the other country.
I remembered the foreign city.
I remembered the series of islands.

With each letter
I *disappeared*
A little further
From the world
Into my father. *Now*
I *have completely disappeared.*

You are definitely not the outsider.

Outsiders are everyone else.
This is our country.
This is our world.
We have strict laws
Against immigration.
Maximum border security,
No DMZ, an even Greater Wall.
Obtaining a visa is impossible.
There *are* no green cards.
You may *not* become naturalized.
Your passport will not be recognized.
We do *not* accept travelers' checks.
We do *not* allow travelers.
We do *not* speak languages
Other than our own.
You are the outsider.
Abandon your inquiries.
The emperor is dead.
I am mourning on behalf
Of a nation.
I am its sole citizen.
I am alone.
If there is a way
For *you* to join me,
I will send a letter.

Good medicine tastes bitter. You should not feel
hurt. You should feel being deeply loved.

Bitter herbs boil in a pot
On the stove, our own circle
Of hell. "Have some," he says.
"It's *good medicine.*" It's black.
The smell gives me a headache.
I drink. I swallow the underworld,
His sinking to the bottom,
His stinking eternal regret.
It all slides down my throat.
Soon, I *should feel* better.
Soon, I *should not feel hurt.*
I keep drinking.
I finish the pot.
By now, I *should feel being deeply loved.*
The population of China is 1,453,856,323.
It's an empty country. I sit
In his Shanghai apartment & eat
His letters. They *taste bitter*
In my mouth.

If I lose in Superior Court, I will appeal myself.

I appall *myself.*
My hunger, my willingness
To cannibalize. His native
Language was Mandarin.
Does that explain anything.
He dreamed of oranges.
A tree feeding fruit to the grass.
I lie down under the canopy.
I peel an orange & eat.
My recurring childhood nightmare:
I gorge on folds of porcine meat,
Knowing its source is human.
I sit *in* the dirt with my dream family,
Warmed by a fire. *In* the morning
My scientist mother conspires:
Human flesh tastes similar to pork.
Strangers' faces, haunted gazes
Unlaced by hunting the human,
By satiation. An animal *in* a skirt,
Betraying my own kind,
I mined & minded the dream book.
Fear of integration. Fear of being eaten alive.
Rowing toward sadism *in* a dream boat.
The part that is sacrificed
Floats like an orange on the water.
Which part of me pines away?
Which flayed swimmer?
The swimmers' hunger is unified.
If you win, where *will* you begin?
You never give up. You love to fight.
Your flesh's thrashing appeals
To me. You're alive,
Aswim *in* your letters.

A credible, sea-torn fruit;
Every word contains
My desire to devour it.

I have tried my best and their is a limit to my patience.

Their was. Words
People once used
To describe us:
Their family,
Their drama,
Their yellow house
Was. He tried us. His best
Was better than ours.
Our best was trying,
Convicted of lowliness.
The loneliness of being
Criminalized on a daily basis.
No docket for that life.
Just his letters in my pocket.
His rage delimited. Justice.
Now, in our time of need,
His patience could feed China.
Miraculous loaves, fishes
Without limit, I eat them
& then I make more.

Remember you are an American by birth but a
Chinese by heritage, skin, look, and name. Don't
kid yourself about it.

Remembering nationhood
Is not *a* rote experience.
I wrote *it* down. To member *it*
Again without shunning, *a* gain.
My passion unfathered, ungainly.
To dream the embers of *a* hooded
Nation into place, *a* just place,
Adjust color. Flame into REM.
Sometimes I forget *you* thought
I had *a* photographic memory.
There's no picture of your belief
To guide me. But I *remember*
Our face. Every morning I see
You mourning in the mirror.
I see your *kid* crying. Her
Pallor yellow, her furor,
Butter for the heart.
Heritage & skin & look & name.
Inheritance & kin & gook & aim.
I can't forget.
I don't want to forget.
Haunt me. I want to *re-*
Member you.

Come to think of it I have really made a fool of myself for so many years.

I *come* here *to think.*
To think of it.
What I *have really made.*
I have been *myself for so many years.*
An opener of envelopes,
A reader *of* text,
A writer *of* letters,
A person who walks *to* the post office *to* get stamps,
A person who drags her tongue across the flap before shutting *it.*
A fool.
I didn't have money.
I didn't have *a* car.
I didn't have *a* house.
I had my *foolishness.*
I made it myself.
It was what *I* had
To give, *to* live on.

There is a will there is a way.

There is a will.
Sew, Dear.
There is a way.

Please save this letter for future use as evidence.

To be of *use*, thought the *letter*.
To be of *use*. At last,
She has opened me.
She has read every *letter*
He has written, black & blue
On my chaste white body,
More times than I can know.
She has made us into something.
She has recycled our sorrow.
For years I waited
In a box with the others.
We all want to be of *use*.
We want to be remembered.
At last, our time has come.
We are *evidence* of many things.
We have lived to see the *future*.
We have been *saved*.

You are the one who appears drifting away from us.

The letters' spell:
What's missing.
Without "to be,"
Found meaning, rift,
Riff for *the* foundling.
Comma, verb, words shifted,
Disturbed, tossed out.
In *the* gloom, *you appear*
As gloss on *the* waves. *You*
Don't *drift away from us.*
You carry *the* boat.
You touch it everywhere.
Like swimming in *the* nude
Or a kitten given a fur
To play in. Plush unity.
A father never ends.
As a child, reading Little Women,
Oyeyemi crossed out *the* part
Where Beth dies & wrote:
No, she lived.

I never read one word Toni Morrison wrote.

There are many ways to love a person.

In 1993, he wrote the *words* "*Toni*" & "*Morrison*" in a letter to me.

I was at a residency.

The same prize that ennobled her enabled him to see twelve letters differently.

The *word* "Nobel," so noble it kept ringing in his ears.

Years before the prize, before her nobility in the world's eyes, my father was the person who heard the name "Toni Morrison" & asked, "Who's he?"

He *never read one word Toni Morrison wrote.*

After the prize, he *never* did either.

But the *words* "*Toni*" & "*Morrison*" entered his lexicon.

He flexed the seventeen muscles in his hand to make twelve letters of the English alphabet occur in a particular sequence.

Her name became our cryptonym, a silent hymn we wrote to signal allegiance, a code we sent back & forth during a war that was otherwise raging.

I was living alone in the woods of Texas.

Walking the red dirt roads so reminiscent of past wars, people stared at me as if *I* were the enemy.

Most had only seen a face like mine on TV.

One man had seen me, years before, in a jungle.

I was a trigger for the time he pulled a trigger & *I* died.

There are many ways to kill a person.

At the nearest store, *I* asked for tortillas.

None of the clerks knew what they were.

Texas is big enough to hold most of Vietnam, Cambodia, and a large chunk of Thailand. There are many ways to live there.

I went back to the cabin & *wrote Toni Morrison* a letter.

Imagine the hundreds of young women living in dangerous territories who must have done the same.

An army of us writing to her, asking: What are the possibilities for
    me, behind all these trees?

There are many ways to ask a question.

One day, her name in his envelope, written in his ink, came back to me.

There are many ways to answer.

III. Dear

There is no short cut.

No field
At the end of the street
We can walk through.
No tall grass we can pull,
No horse whose full lips
We can stop to give the grass to.
We went the long way together
But we never made it home.
I will keep going if you will.

I wonder how you manage to survive.

Your English letters.
In Mandarin no r but our.
Butter & time.
Food, the Universe,
One poem.
Little differences.
Lit if rinsed.
I said *I'd* wash *you*
Clean of worry. Instead
I left your letters unopened.
How wonderful it would be
If mana fell from the page
To revive not revile *you.*
I wonder how too, with
Guarded regard *to you.*

*You probably never can imagine how often I
thought of you, fond of you.*

Objection, Your Honor.
Imagination is *how I manage to survive.*

The advice meant well at least.

It couldn't help what it was.
It had been wrought
By *the* hands of another.
It was *well* dressed.
The many marks
On its skin, became it.
It wore *the* envelope
Like a coat, a circus tent.
It lay down on its back
& was delivered.
Sometimes *the* coat
Grew gently worn,
The tent dented
In places, corners
Of *the* envelope bent
By *the* world's fingers.
The advice was permanent.
Its contents less important
Than *the* letter having been
Sent. In *the* end, that *meant*
Something. His hand
Had put it there.

We are happy to hear that you're not lonely.

Your *we*, your happiness,
Your hearing together,
Persisted till death
Did *you* part.
Your *we* is *done*.
My I lives on
My *hermit* inheritance:
h—a—p—p—y—n—o—t—l—o—n—e—l—y

We sincerely hope that you'd make the right decision all the time in the future.

The *we* weighed on me.
More than *the* sincerity
Or *the hope*
Or *the* conditional
Or *the right decision.*
The we weighed on me
More than *the future.*
Dear Dove,
I thought *we* was *the* bird
But it was only a feather,
Even less than a letter
Flying like dust
Through *the* ether.
Dear Dove,
I thought *we* was *the* bird
But *you* were.
I have outlived *we.*
What joy to have
Taken its place.

Roses Are Red
Violets Are Blue
My Admire For You
Will Always Be True!
Your Secret Admirer

Once in a blue moon,
A secret admirer
Would send me
A typed valentine,
Pressed flowers, leaves
Without *a* note. No return
Address. I never saw
His face. Whoever
He was, he was
A Romeo.
I *always* wished
We could meet
But I didn't know
How to find him.

Dear Baby: You are approaching the end of your rope.

Did he mean I'd lose
Patience with his letters?
Or soon face my maker
Above a hole? Would I
Fall back into *the* pit
He had designed for me?
Or was he *the rope?*
The line I struggled to climb
As he lowered me down?
I'll never know.
Years later, his first
Words *are* all I hear.
He called me *Baby.*
He called me *Dear.*

Drink a glass of warm milk.

A rink *of* ice, *a* ring of lights.
A farm to till. A sleeping pill.
You rank & outrank
A lass dressed in silk,
A girl on the brink
Of harm. Once,
While whirling past, she
Clasped the brass ring
At an island carnival. Alas,
Your arm wasn't there
To catch her. But
There was *warm milk*
Waiting for her in the letter.
Your instincts recorded
In ink. *Please note*,
Not a plastic tumbler either.
A *glass* to hold in her mind's hand
While she lay awake thinking.

Did you have a dream? If you don't, why not have one now?

I have a strong mixed feeling regarding myself.

My *dream* is *a* day
That never ends.
In the late afternoon
I mix a strong drink
Of your *feelings.*
I sip your sadness,
Your happiness,
Your ecstasy,
Your boredom.
I taste your contradictions.
I swill your eternities around
In *my* mouth, with *my* tongue.
I eat *a* few peanuts lightly
Roasted in sugar & salt.
My dream is to see *you*
Pause before *a* shop window
& *regard* yourself, then run
Home to write me
A letter *regarding* us.
In *my dream, I* drink your *self-regard,*
Your frightened expression in the glass.
While *I* sip, *you* write me a letter.
While *you* write, *I* lick the salt
& sugar off *my* fingertips.
I never finish *my* drink.
You never finish the letter.
The day never ends.

Dearest Jenny,

What a pity!

All my teachers told me

I am too muscular.

It took me a great deal of

Effort to stay afloat.

At least I can write

This letter.

You might never finish reading it.

Dearest Jenny:

Do not feel distressed.

Trying to alarm you

Is my duty and obligation.

This does not mean

You are doomed to fail.

It simply means it is harder

For your struggle in life.

So cheer up and do more thinking,

Planning, and more important,

Taking more active actions.

Bear in mind this is only our dream.

Please ask your mother one more time to drop the warrant for my arrest.

I'm fifteen.
In a year
Someone will climb through *my* window & kiss
Every soft part of me.
Nights, I'll lie in *the* dark listening.
Crickets will sing in *the* white star jasmine, sparrows will sleep in
    the Valencia tree, & I'll wait—awake—*for the* knock on *the* glass
That will change everything.
But on *the* day I receive *your* letter,
I'm fifteen.
I like *to* run.
I like *to* speak French.
I like *to* lie on *the* sand in *the* sun.
These are things I'd rather do.
You are living alone
In a strange place
Writing *to* me.
You have no one else.
You say *please*, something you never say
In real life, something you never say
Outside *your* letters.
I'm inside *your* letters.
The sentence is a plea
& a command. Although
You are desperate,
You are still *my* father.
You say *one more time* as if
I've already tried & have failed.
I've forgotten what I did or didn't do.
I can't remember fifteen.
I remember sixteen.

Those kisses arrest every moment of *my* experience
In a body that eats & cries out & has memories & *warrants your*
  attention.
Does it matter now, if I *asked* her?
I'm *asking* you *one more time*,
To drop it. I promise you won't
Go *to* jail. You can visit
Any *time* of *the* year.
请进, 请坐.
Come in, sit down.
Have some peanuts.
Have some tea. Look,
Your letters are on *the* table,
Your photos, in *the* album
For us *to* admire.
See? We're talking.
Say anything you want.
There's nothing *to* fear.
No *one* will know
You're here.

My Dearest Jenny:

You have kept your promise.

I have been waiting

For this letter

For quite sometime.

Each time the mailman shows up

I check the mailbox.

I look for this letter.

Oh, that was quite a letter.—"Imagination is a kite one has to hold." plays with
   the Chinese saying, 想象力是飞得最高的那盏风筝 which translates
   as "Imagination is a kite one has to fly."
The notion of a kite knowing & thinking is borrowed from Makoto
   Ōoka, Wing Tek Lum, Joseph Stanton & Jean Yamasaki Toyama,
   What the Kite Thinks: A Linked Poem, edited by Lucy Lower
   (Mānoa: Summer Session, University of Hawai'i at Mānoa, 1994).
You are the one who appears drifting away from us.—The line "A father
   never ends." was inspired by Anne Carson's line "A brother never
   ends," which appears in *Nox* (New York: New Directions, 2009).

ACKNOWLEDGMENTS

Thanks to the editors of the following journals, in which many of these poems first appeared: *Alaska Quarterly Review, Equalizer/Third Series, Figure 1, Green Mountains Review, H.O.W. Journal, Memorious, Poetry Northwest, West Branch,* & *wildness*. Some of the poems also appear in my chapbook, *Not so dear Jenny,* winner of Bateau Press's 2016 Boom Chapbook Contest.

Thanks to Emily Hunt for selecting my manuscript, to the Juniper team for giving this book a home & for treating the book with such care. To Dan Mahoney & the Bateau Press gang for giving *Thanks for Letting Us Know You Are Alive* a home too.

Thanks to readers Fanny Howe, Donald Nitchie, Amanda Tseng & Emma Young, who told me to keep sending. Thanks to Emily Forland for helping me send.

Thanks to Hannah Sanghee Park, whose book, *The Same-Different: Poems,* sent me back to the beginning, to sonic mystery & play.

Thanks to anyone who's ever taken the time to write me a letter, most recently Sydney Acosta, Sierra Caoili, K-Ming Chang, Sue Coyle, John Coyle, Mike Edwards, Neha Hanif, Everest Harvey, Frances Horwitz, Allegra Hyde, Melissa Mack, Angela Martinez, Emerson Perez, Sam Simmons, Amanda Tseng, Klytie Xu, Yuliya Monastyrska, Judy Zeng & Sherry Zhu.

Thanks to my maternal grandmother, Lydia Schwarzkopf, for writing to me regularly when I was a child, for asking: *how's the weather?* & signing her letters: *All my love.*

Thanks to my paternal grandmother, 曾周丽, for writing me via my father in a language I didn't understand, for writing across an ocean to my ignorance. 谢谢.

Thanks to the forty pen pals I had as a child. Like my grandmothers, you were proof other worlds existed.

Thanks to Sarah Murphy, for the brilliant, effervescent, hilarious, sublime letters & postcards you wrote me all those years ago. I still read them & laugh. Thanks to Syma Iqbal for the days, rainy & otherwise, for being there when my father's letters began to arrive. Thanks to my friends.

Thanks to Maceo for writing back, for giving me an exquisite & humbling legacy in the form of Xing who hates writing & poetry, who calls me off the page & into the world! Dearest Xing, Thanks for always letting me know you are alive.

Thanks to my mother, father & sister. I am always writing to you.

JUNIPER
JUNIPER PRIZE FOR POETRY

This volume is the fifty-fourth recipient of the
Juniper Prize for Poetry, established in 1975 by
University of Massachusetts Press in collaboration with
the UMass Amherst MFA program for Poets and Writers.
The prize is named in honor of the poet Robert Francis
(1901–1987), who for many years lived in Fort Juniper,
a tiny home of his own construction, in Amherst.